Sharon —

DELIGHTFUL!

Fantastic to "meet"
you —

I AM SURE 2013
will be great for
Both of us!

Best Wishes.

Mo

Heroic HR A little book with BIG ideas

. . . The **Arch of HR Triumph** and other inspirational thoughts and actions involving **Human Resources** and its use of **technology**

Marc S. Miller

Heroic HR

A little book with BIG ideas

Published by Futura Publishing LLC
6205 Bull Creek Road
Austin, Texas 78757-2701 USA

ISBN: 978-0-9789397-3-1

Dedication

This little book is dedicated to all the HR Heroes throughout the world who keep the wheels of the public and private sector turning everyday by handling the challenging tasks of human capital management with or without the help of technology.

Acknowledgements

To Al Walker, Sid Simon, Joe Pickler, Julie Mann, Larry Hall, Carol Wiese, Pam Puetz and Tom Faulkner (my editor and publisher), who like me, have given their all to HR technology and who helped me with the concept and execution of this "little" book.

To the special people in my life who are all of these: family, friends and clients – from all places near and far. And to Sam Martin – who gave me the positive "energy" to move this effort along.

You will find this book meaningful if you are...

- A senior leader of HR in your organization;

- Working in the function of HR at your company, and wishing things were done easier and quicker;

- An IT person who wishes HR would go away and not bother you daily with IT issues; or,

- A HR technology service provider who wants a painless way to better communicate with HR folks who might end up being a new customer.

You should definitely read this little book because...

- It brings you up-to-date on what HR technology enables you to apply to the work that is done by Human Resources professionals.

- It gives you the arguments to help you justify any reasonable expenses needed to make it happen.

- It helps you build your case and gain executive sponsorship for any HR technology initiatives.

- Provides you with "helpful hints" along with specific details to guide you through a Needs Analysis and HR technology software vendor evaluation initiative.

How you will benefit from this "little book"….

- Doesn't take long to read!!

- Summarizes the state of HR administration; where it came from and what is achievable **now**.

- Sets up the "talking points" for you to build your case for $$$$$ for projects.

- Gives you a "vision" or a strategy that you can sell internally.

- Gives you readily digestible information at a reasonable level of detail that will cause others to see you as the HR technology visionary that I hope you strive to be (or already are)!

- And hopefully, transfers the passion for a strategic HR role in your organization from me to you.

Contents

The purpose of this little book:

Presenting **BIG** ideas and
thought-provoking views . . .

. . . concerning how the function of Human Resources can act **heroically** by providing superior, effective and proven results through the use of **technologies**.

*"**Heroic HR** is the outcome of a strategic HR function combined with an effective, supportive HR technology delivering extraordinary results to all stakeholders."*

– Marc S. Miller – speech, IHRIM Conference, 2006

*"Information responsibility, then, begins with correctly identifying the information you need to effectively carry out your job, and extends to ensuring that the **information flows to people** in other areas who stand to benefit from it, and in a form in which those people will readily understand it.*

*"...Increasingly, however, the measure of the executive will **not** be his/her ability to interpret **data**, but his/her ability to define and exploit **information.**"*

– Peter Drucker, Across the Board, December 1991

What is a "Hero?"

A **Hero** provides the
right action at the
right time and place . . .
to produce an
extraordinary result!

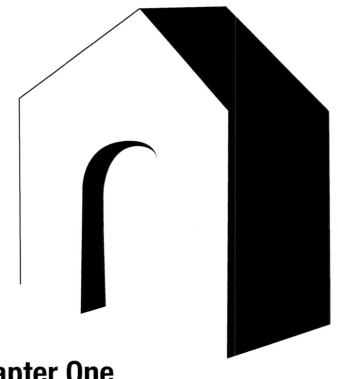

Chapter One
HR's **Evolving** Role . . .

. . . how the function of HR must **reinvent itself**

This is where HR has been and is **moving forward** from →

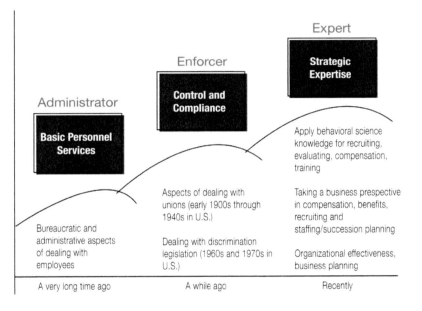

Expert

Enforcer

**Strategic
Expertise**

Administrator

**Control and
Compliance**

**Basic Personnel
Services**

Apply behavioral science
knowledge for recruiting,
evaluating, compensation,
training

Aspects of dealing with
unions (early 1900s through
1940s in U.S.)

Taking a business prespective
in compensation, benefits,
recruiting and
staffing/succession planning

Bureaucratic and
administrative aspects
of dealing with
employees

Dealing with discrimination
legislation (1960s and 1970s in
U.S.)

Organizational effectiveness,
business planning

A very long time ago   A while ago   Recently

This is what
HR is (has been)
comfortable
doing and
providing ➔

"TRANSACTIONS"
"ADMINISTRIVIA"

- Policies / Programs / Rules and Forms

- Staffing / Recruiting

- Employee Relations

- Staff Development

- Performance Appraisals

- Compensation

- Benefits Administration

- Communications

- "Life Event" Processing

Unfortunately,
this is how HR
in a corporation
is often **perceived**

→

Value

"Only 10% of current HR contributions add value. The other 90% is transactional nonsense.**"**

Jac Fitz-Enz, former Director of Saratoga Institute

This is how
HR as a function
in a corporation
should be
perceived →

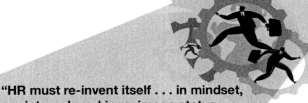

"HR must re-invent itself . . . in mindset, internal workings, image status, organizational position and capacity to initiate, manage change and add value."

Value

Work in America Institute: The Partnership Paradigm for Competitive Advantage

This what
HR needs to
achieve in an
organization ➜

Strive to Become Viewed as
a Strategic Business Partner

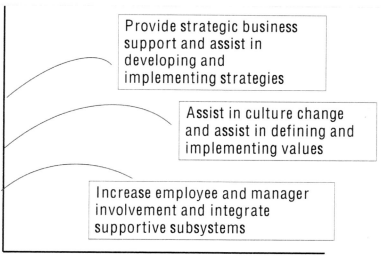

Provide strategic business support and assist in developing and implementing strategies

Assist in culture change and assist in defining and implementing values

Increase employee and manager involvement and integrate supportive subsystems

Create Actual Value to
Senior Executives

This is how
HR can create
value in an
organization →

- Ensuring the availability of human capital by **attracting**, **developing** and **retaining** the best knowledge workers;

- **Reducing costs** by providing operational effectiveness;

- Aligning HR's mission/vision to help support and deliver the **organization's strategies**; and,

- Serving as a role model for **reducing costs** and **achieving operational excellence**.

These are the
hot button issues
which HR must be in
a position to support,
administer or even solve
in an effective way
(to become **Heroic**)

→

- **Attracting** and **retaining** a talented workforce;

- **Developing leaders** and establishing succession;

- Providing support and tools for **work group collaboration** representing differing organizational components and staff; and,

- Supporting work group production from anywhere in the world, at any time.

This is a
Guru quote ➔

*"HR should **not** be defined by what it does, but by what it **delivers** – that results in enriching the organization's **value**."*

– Dave Ulrich, University of Michigan

This is what
the CEO, the
Board of Directors,
and other Stakeholders
expect from HR ➔

- Administrative efficiencies resulting in cost reduction;
- Leadership and support in implementing business strategies;
- Quality of services to all customers;
- Responsiveness;
- Risk management;
- Talent acquisition and pipeline; and,
- Effective leveraging of technology to all appropriate functions within the realm of HR, Payroll and Benefits.

Value Creation!

This is the **classical** depiction of how HR should attempt to transform itself ➡️

HR Transformation . . .
the Classical View

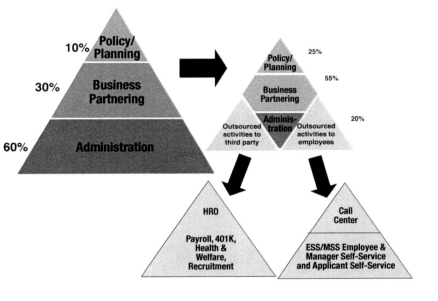

And this shows the organizational **building blocks** needed to **accomplish** the transformation ➔

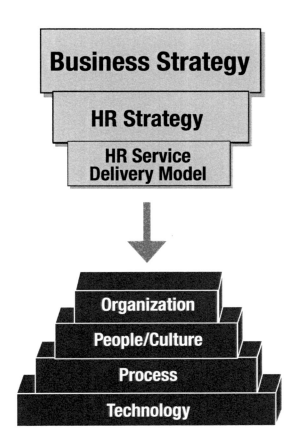

The Strategic Triangle of the classical

HR Service Delivery Model △▲

combined with the 4 Building Blocks

(including new HR technology) results

in a new **structure** – a **tribute** to a

strategically oriented HR function

➡

The Arch of HR Triumph

The Columns

- Employee and manager self-service (ESS/MSS) delivers efficencies.

- Cycle time is reduced.

- Data ownership instilled.

- Accuracy improved, input tracked.

- Workflow driven, "Best Practices" built in.

- Outsource non-core activities to firms that do it best.

- Call center utilization if needed.

The Arch of HR Triumph

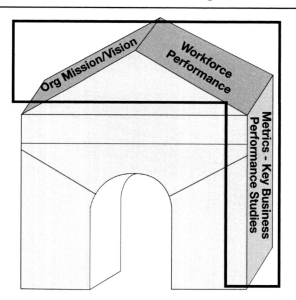

The Shell

- Corporate Mission and Vision is always in sight.

- Metrics support the transition **from "Data Management" to "Information Craftsmanship."**

- Metrics presented graphically, showing trends.

- Workforce analytics captures competency gaps.

- Future states shown with modeling within Metrics.

- Key Performance Indices (KPI) provided by HR enhances strategic positioning.

The Arch of HR Triumph

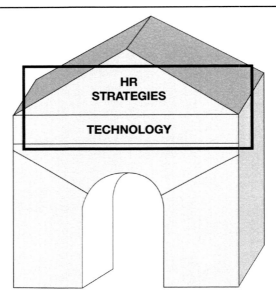

The Pinnacle

- HR strategy in support of overall organization strategies.
- HR technology service delivery strategy supports HR strategy and objectives.
- Web delivery results in 24/7 access from multiple devices.
- Delivery by "Cloud" computing, Software-as-a-Service (SaaS).
- As a result of aligned strategic components and collaborative Mission and Visions, the HR function will no longer be an isolated function, and it will be viewed as a Strategic Business Partner.

The Arch of HR Triumph

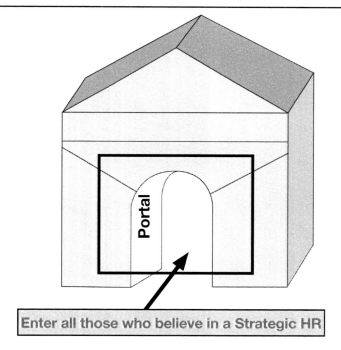

Portal

Enter all those who believe in a Strategic HR

The Portal

- Fully realized and integrated **into the organization's intranet** – "MyPortal" – for every employee.

- Strong communications tool.

- Accounts for and considers Change Management issues.

- Critical component needed to **manage adaptability of "best practice" workflows** within the delivery of ESS/MSS.

- **All content owned or reviewed and provided by HR.**

Chapter Two
Nightmarish thoughts . . .

...keeping

HR folks

awake.

These are some **issues**, **questions** and **concerns** that HR folks have on their minds

- How do I create more value for my organization?

- How do I better measure effectiveness of the HR function? Of our workforce?

- How do I achieve the positioning of HR as a **strategic partner**?

- How do I get and keep everyone within HR (and within the company) on the same page?

- How do I use the Web and other technologies to help me keep doing more with less staff – and still keep up with all the required governmental and internal reporting deadlines?

These are some
key questions
that need to be asked,
answered and resolved
to ease their minds

(and help HR folks have a restful night's sleep)

- Is my HR organization delivering what the business needs to successfully implement our strategy and return a **profit** to the shareholders?

- Is my credibility, and the credibility of HR, where it should be?

- Do I have the right people in HR who can handle new roles and responsibilities?

- Is HR nimble enough, flexible enough, to respond to changing organizational strategies?

- Have we created processes that **optimize our investments** in HR technologies?

These are some **critical questions** about **technology** that must also be asked, answered and resolved

(that certainly contribute to sleepless nights, if they are not)

→

- Does our current HR service delivery technology work?

- Is the way we use HR technology today cost-effective – and in **alignment** with corporate strategies and culture?

- Do we even have the right HR technology in place now?

- Are our HR technologies properly integrated?

- Are we happy with our current HRT vendor(s)?

- What about our **Web utilization**? Are we doing the best we can using its power? For the company? For HR services?

- Are HR technology efforts/plans linked with and supportive of other company-wide initiatives, in other functions?

- What should our policy be regarding **social media**? What role does HR and HR technology play in this?

HR will be perceived as **heroic** and deserving of a parade through the **Arch of HR Triumph** by delivering quantifiable results resolving (among others) this key concern

- How do my current HR service technology capabilities, including underlying software applications, Web utilization, existing outsourcing providers, workflow and best practices, help me support my stakeholders' **hot button** issues while at the same time continue to **create value**?

Additionally,
if used correctly,
HR technology
applications can
result in gaining
significant
information
related to answering
these questions ➡️

- Are our employees learning? How? How quickly? How effectively?

- Are our managers managing effectively?

- Do I have the right people in the right job, doing the right things at the right time? Are we paying them accordingly?

- What happens when a "key employee" leaves? Do we know where replacements come from? Do we even have them? Is there a "succession plan" in place?

- Wait, do we even know who or what is a "key employee?" Do we track skills and competencies? Do we adequately track employee performance?

- Is the HR function contributing to **value creation** and **shareholder return** by providing timely, effective administrative services and new program development and delivery?

- Do these programs directly support our **corporate strategies** (i.e. "hot buttons")?

Chapter Three

Technology:
Using it to help achieve **Heroics**

or…

How I learned

enough about

HR technology

to hold a drink and

chat about it.

These are issues and topics that HR should be interested in finding out about relating to **HR Service Delivery** technologies ➡

- What functions do I **outsource**? How do I find out what makes sense?

- What is the difference between an ASP vendor and a **SaaS** (Software-as-a-Service) vendor?

- What service level agreements (**SLAs**) do I insist upon?

- How much should I **budget** for new HR technology? How do I find out the range of costs?

- What is our HR **Web strategy** or presence? How does it link to the company's overall Web focus?

These are some issues and topics related to the HR technology **big picture** environment that might be puzzling HR folks ➔

- I've spent many millions implementing an ERP (e.g., PeopleSoft, Oracle, SAP or others) but am I getting the **value** out of its use? How can I find out?

- Do I bother with an **upgrade** to a major release, or do I consider other options?

- How do I get **different** software applications and platforms and technology talking to each other?

- Which vendors provide the best value for functionality, delivery and **customer support**?

In times of **mergers** and **acquisitions**, this is a question causing puzzlement among HR (and other) folks high up in the organization ➤

- We just announced a merger with (or acquired) "Company B." We utilize **Vendor A** for HR, Benefits and Payroll; they have **Vendor B**, now what?

In fact, these situations may also lead to a **change** in HR Service Delivery technologies →

- A purchase of an **ERP**, or upgrade;

- The purchase of a HR-related Web-based application;

- New initiatives involving related outsourcing or insourcing evaluations;

- A new **CHRO**;

- A new **CIO**;

- A new **CEO**; or,

- A significant change to, or within, your current HR technology provider, such as a merger or acquisition or **product discontinuance**.

This is a list of
outcomes
resulting from
the effective use
of HR technologies
→

- ## Cost Reduction
  Significant improvements in cost of delivering HR services on a per employee per month (PEPM) basis

- ## Cycle Time Reduction
  In business process and transaction completion – from "trigger event" to conclusion

- ## Improved Information
  Translating "data" to metrics and trends, and then to **best practices**

- ## Increased Capabilities
  New organization programs in response to employee feedback and business performance metrics showing trends

- ## Increased Commitment
  By improved outreach, via targeted programs over the Web

- ## Faster Changes
  By designing and delivering systems quicker to react to organizational pressure and change faster

Here are the many **key features** and **functions** of an effective HR technology capability ➔

HRT Features and Functions

- Web delivered – SaaS – "Software-as-a-Service"

- Employee Self-Service and Manager Self-Service (ESS/MSS) – Web-delivered – "MyPortal," Manager's "in box"

- Best practices and workflow built-in, with templates provided

- E-mail triggers and notification for action alerts and process steps

- Functionality encompassing most functions within HR including Payroll and Benefits

- A comprehensive "library of standard reports"

- Ad hoc Report Writer (user oriented)

- Metrics and "Dashboard" – graphically presented

- "Drill down" capability – underlying data at a click

- Tables – changeable/manageable by end user or by trained "power user"

- Effective date processing – future and retroactive

- Security based on rules and end-user roles

Here are some
of the ways
companies
are **creating value**
using these
Web-based features →

Employee Self-Service for:

- Benefits plan enrollments/changes
- Retirement and pension planning, status and fund allocations
- Life event changes triggering follow-up actions
- Access to individual vacation and sick day balances

Manager Self-Service for:

- Direct reports' Performance Management and Succession Planning
- Budgeting
- Approvals and authorizations – "in box" action items
- Staff scheduling

Forecasts and Trends based on historical data analysis – resulting in anticipatory programs

These are more
Web-delivered
HR initiatives that
will **increase**
efficiencies and
effectiveness
throughout an
organization ➜

- Web-delivered **time capture** and reporting

- Web-delivered **performance** and career development

- Web-delivered job posting and employment application and recruitment process – **onboarding**

- Web-based **work group** collaboration

- Web-based remote location access to whatever is needed, 24/7, with **smartphones** and **tablets**

- **Dashboards** and **metrics** for executive- and manager-level decision support

Speaking of
Dashboards
and **Metrics** →

What do we (HR)
have to think about in
order to capture and
present **meaningful
information** in the form
of Metrics depicted on a
Dashboard?

And further our
reputation of providing
strategic, valued
information.

Here are some traditional **financial** based Metrics of interest to a Board of Directors or Executive Committee ➔

HR folks, you should know of these.

Cash Flow Report-Cash Inflows and Outflows
- Demonstrates a company's ability to generate cash.
- Shows the company's ability to meet financial obligations and pay dividends.
- Identifies potential needs for additional financing.
- Assesses the effects of cash and noncash and financial transactions.

Income Statement-Revenues, Expenses and Resulting Net Income or Loss over a period of time
- Sales = Revenues
- Net Sales = Gross Sales - Sales Returns and Allowance
- Gross Margin = Net Sales - Cost of Goods Sold
- Operating Income (Loss) = Gross Margin - Operating Expenses
- Income Before Taxes = Operating Income (Loss) +- Other Income (Expenses)

Balance Sheet-Information on what is owned (assets), what is owed (liabilities) and shareholders equity in the business.
- Assets
    - » Current Assets: Cash, Marketable Securities, Inventory, Accounts Receivable, Prepaid expenses
    - » Noncurrent Assets: Land, Plant, Equipment, Leasehold improvements,Investments, Goodwill
- Liabilities
    - » Current Liabilities: Accounts payable, Accrued Liabilities, Taxes Payable, Notes Payable, Short-Term Debt, Total Current Liabilities
    - » Noncurrent Liabilities: Bonds and Mortgages, Notes Payable, Deferred Taxes
- Shareholders Equity; Preferred and Common Stock, retained earnings

Here are some **traditional overall business** performance Metrics showing **value creation** that are of interest to a Board of Directors or Executive Committee ➔

HR folks, you should at least know what they mean.

Return on Investments (ROI)

Any ratio that measures the return on a given investment.

Return on Equity (ROE)

The ratio of net earnings to shareholder equity. Tells shareholders how well the business has used their money to generate a return.

Return on Assets (ROA)

The ratio of net earnings to total assets. Reflects the profitability of all of an organizations resources.

Return on Net Assets (RONA)

The ratio of net earnings to net assets. Calculates profitability at the business unit level.

Return on Capital Employed (ROCE)

The ratio of net earnings, plus after-tax interest on long term debt, to shareholders equity plus long term debt. Used as a comparison among several companies.

Here are some common **Human Capital** oriented Metrics showing the ROI of the "people asset" for an organization. ➜

HR folks, keep an eye on all of these and present them on a scorecard or dashboard (over time).

Human Capital Revenue Factor (HCRF)
- Total Revenue / Full Time Equivalent (FTE)

Human Economic Value Added (HEVA)
- (Net Operating Margin – Cost of Capital) / Full Time Equivalent (FTE)

Human Capital Cost Factor (HCCF)
- W2 Pay + Cost of Contingent Labor + Cost of Absenteeism + Cost of Turnover

Human Capital Value Added (HCVA)
- Operating Revenue – (Operating Expenses – Pay and Benefits) / FTEs

Human Capital Return on Investment (HCROI)
- Operating Revenue – (Operating Expenses – Pay and Benefits) / Pay and Benefits

Here are some "pure" **Human Resources metrics** that can be provided in some form or another (preferably graphically) to HR's "stakeholders"

	Expressed As	**Computed As**
Work Force Productivity	Net income/ee	$\dfrac{\text{Net Income}}{\text{Total Active Employees}}$
	Production Output (per employee)	$\dfrac{\text{\#Units Output/Hourly Employee}}{\text{Total Hourly Active Employees}}$
	Dollars of Sales (per employee)	$\dfrac{\text{Dollar Value or Units Sold}}{\text{Total \# of Active Employees}}$
Compensation	Benefits Costs as % of Payroll	$\dfrac{\text{Cost of Benefits}}{\text{Total Payroll}}$
	Average Total Yrly Compensation/ Exempt employee	$\dfrac{\text{Total Exempt Compensation}}{\text{Total \# Exempt Employees}}$
Cost of Hire	Hiring Cost/Exempt employee	$\dfrac{\text{Total Hiring Cost Exempt EEs}}{\text{\# of Exempt Employees Hired}}$

Here is a suggested **HR Scorecard** presenting these metrics →

HR folks, it is even more ideal to present them graphically and as a future trend – BUT one step at a time.

Acquisition
- Cost per hire
- Time to fill jobs
- Total number of new hires
- Total number of replacement staff
- Quality of new hires

Financial
- Total labor cost as a percentage of operating expense
- Average pay per employee
- Benefits cost as a percent of pay
- Average performance score as compared to revenue per FTE
- Human Economic Value Added (HEVA)

Retention
- Total separation rate
- Percentage of voluntary separation to total separations
- Separations by length of service
- Percentage of separations among "key" performers
- Cost of turnover

Development
- Training cost as a percentage of payroll
- Total training hours provided
- Average number of hours of training per FTE
- Training hours by functions
- Training ROI

Service
- Employee satisfaction levels
- Management satisfaction levels
- Percentage of transactions using ESS

Process Quality
- Accuracy in data recording
- Response time per request

Here are a few samples of an effective **dashboard presentation** (enabled with HR technology) ➔

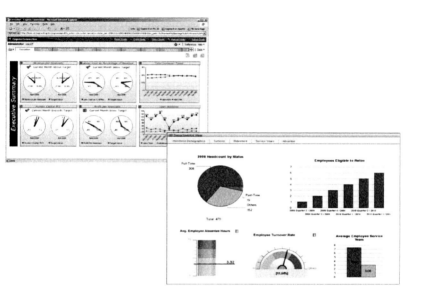

I know, I know, this is black/white, but you should create them as **colorful, eye-catching graphics** that are **self-explanatory** and **show trends**.

Here are **four** **rules** of choosing and presenting effective Metrics.

Source: BLR.com – White Paper "HR Metrics: How to Measure and Communicate Your Strategic Value in Bottom-Line Terms," Ronald Adler and Jennifer Burdick

- Organizations **measure what they treasure**.

- What gets measured gets **done**.

- Critical metrics have an **owner**.

- To have value, metrics should have **a target to be compared to**.

This **sums up**
"Heroic HR"
initiatives
using technologies
as a potential
mission/vision or
goal statement ➔

A mission statement for HR initiatives:

"Radically improve the value, effectiveness and cost structure of HR, through the use of technologically-rich solutions that fundamentally alter the way HR provides strategic advice, expertise and administrative services to employees and managers."

– Marc S. Miller, 2011 speech to Ultimate Software Users Group

Chapter Four

Accomplishing the goal and **getting it done** . . .

…suggested **next steps** based on lessons learned.

This is a (short) list of suggested **action items** that should work in your organization →

- Talk to senior management and discuss their view of HR's current environment and ability to **create value**.

- Examine your HR goals, objectives, resources and adjust to **support organization direction**, **mission** and **vision**.

- Review the capability of your own staff to comprehend, support and sell the concepts of a more strategic HR and related technology upgrades or initiatives.

- Partner with your counterparts in Information Technology, (not just HR Information Systems).

- Understand the organization's overall Web strategy.

Here is a list of **activities** and **tools** that you may need to help you move a "Needs Analysis," HR technology evaluation and selection project forward ➜

Your tool kit
(forms, etc. that you might need)

- Formal project team structure, roles and time commitments.

- Questionnaires to guide your discussion, or to be filled out by senior staff – I call them the "visionaries."

- Questionnaires to guide your discussion or to be filled out in advance by those who perform the day-to-day activities within the realm of HR function. I call them the "Do'ers."

    Note: The questionnaires should include the current "AS IS" environment for each process or activity or function. But just as importantly they should provide thinking points to get the reaction of the interviewee as to the "TO BE," functionality they need for improvement. A list of the features/ functions of a "model" (generic) HR technology capability would be useful.

- Translate the requirements statements into actual questions to selected vendors as the major content of an RFP.

- Proposal evaluation criteria, and scoring schema.

- Onsite demo agenda and time blocks.

- Demo evaluation and scoring tools.

- Due diligence activities – vendor client reference checklist.

Here is a list of initial **evaluation factors** that you can inform the vendors (in the RFP) that you will use to determine the selected HR technology provider

Initial and high level evaluation criteria

FACTOR NAME*	DESCRIPTION
Functionality	Overall degree of fit. Ability to meet YOUR COMPANY's functional requirements: HR, Payroll, and Benefits. This will be based on product demos and not just the RFP responses.
Cost	Overall cost of the Agreement is considered reasonable and within YOUR COMPANY'S expectations.
Ease of Use/Look and Feel	Overall ease-of-use of the application. Specifically in terms of Web-based ESS and MSS, navigation, and the overall usability, and "look and feel."
Implementation and Post-Implementation Services	Overall perception of the vendor's implementation approach and ongoing customer/client support.
Stability of Vendor Organization	Overall financial stability and reputation of the vendor organization.

*Note: various "weights" can be applied to the above factors.

Here is a "Table of Contents" of a **well received*** Request for Proposal (RFP) document ➔

* Vendors eagerly participated in the process and later felt that the process was **fair, balanced** and gave them a **good opportunity** to explain and position their product offerings.

Table of Contents of a
proven Request for Proposal (RFP)

ADDENDUM/ATTACHMENTS

EXCEL SPREADSHEET OF FUNCTIONAL REQUIREMENTS

    Tab A – VENDOR HISTORY AND QUALIFICATIONS, PRODUCT NAME

    Tab B - BUSINESS REQUIREMENTS – HR, PAYROLL, BENEFITS, OTHERS

    Tab C - GENERAL REQUIRMENTS

    Tab D - TECHNOLOGY, BACK-UP & SECURITY

NON DISCLOSURE AGREEMENT

Here is a list of
helpful hints
and observations
that might prove
meaningful during
your HR technology
evaluation activities
→

Helpful Hints

Company Mission/Vision

- If a company mission / vision exists, use it in the beginning of the RFP, let the vendors know what it is, and how the new HR technology initiative must be in alignment with it or supportive of it.

Project Team Commitment

- During the evaluation and selection process, some weeks the Project Manager will be at a 50 percent level. Other weeks 10 percent. Demo weeks will require an almost full-time commitment.

Executive Sponsor

- Critical to have, usually the highest possible HR executive. Also co-sponsor with IT or Finance executives. Be aware of political ramifications. When in doubt, include or invite executives rather than exclude.

Timing for Proposal Prep by Vendors

- Give vendors at least 3 - 4 weeks to prepare and submit their proposals in response to your RFP.

What Makes An Effective RFP

- Gives the vendor an understanding of the role of HR and related functions; also the history of the company, and your utilization of earlier HR technology.

- The business requirements section should consist of requirement statements transformed into narrative questions.

- Do not allow a simple "Yes" or "No" answer. Give the vendors a "Response Code" so they can self-categorize their answer, (for example: "Y" capability is delivered (no modification needed), "F" – future release, etc.

A few more
helpful hints →

Helpful Hints

Onsite Demo Timing

- Will require at least a day and a half – almost two days to cover all aspects of proposed solution, including "look and feel," navigation, report writer, technology, implementation support, training, as well as all the desired functionality within HR, Benefits Administration, Payroll, et al.

Due Diligence

- You will get references from vendor finalists (not usually in proposal, but once they are told they are a "finalist"). Call them. Also use LinkedIn and other social media to pose queries about vendor performance.

Contract Negotiation

- Get your legal staff involved early. Ask bidding vendors for a "standard contract" as part of the proposal submission. Early pricing is never the final pricing. Once the vendor knows they are one of two finalists, negotiations will bring the price down.

This is a list of vendors considered by Marc S. Miller Associates as **players*** worthy of consideration for some type of HR technology support →

***Proven**, with clients and financial stability.

Some are comprehensive HR/Payroll/Benefits administration providers; others are "niche" or best-of-breed for specific functionality within the realm of HR. Pricing not considered.

(as of spring 2012):

- ADP
- Ceridian
- Checkpoint HR
- Cornerstone
- CumulusHR
- ECI
- Epicor
- Humanic Design
- Infinisource
- Kronos
- Lawson
- NuView
- OneSource Virtual

- Oracle
- Paychex
- Paycom
- PDS
- PeopleStrategy
- SAP
- Successfactors
  (purchased by SAP – Jan 2012)
- SumTotal
- Taleo
  (purchased by Oracle – Feb 2012)
- Ultimate Software
- Workday

SHRM lists nearly 200 HRIS providers!
But these are the vendors that Marc S. Miller Associates believes have a proven product and client base.

This is a list of **lessons learned** gathered from organizations that have embarked on achieving a more strategic (and "heroic") HR initiative ➔

- Vision helps, but **passion** excels.

- Set specific targets to accomplish.

- Look for **low-hanging fruit** and early successes.

- Anticipate and plan for overcoming **resistance to change**.

- Assign your best people to formal team-based actions and tasks; **back-fill** with less experienced staff.

- Insist on **executive sponsorship**.

- **Communicate** appropriately – and often – use the company intranet, if possible.

These are **more lessons learned** specifically about technology, process improvement and the search for cost savings ➜

- A **common** underlying software technology architecture among HR/Payroll/Benefits and Financial applications is **preferable to disparate systems**.

- A user friendly – **intuitive** – minimal training needed – end-user graphical interface (GUI) will prove to be a real plus for early adoption and a relatively problem free "go-live."

- Seek a **quick win** and a "foothold" by focusing on processes with the greatest opportunity for success, processes that are visible and perceived as "needing improvement."

- Stay as close to **vanilla** as possible. Take advantage of how the vendor has incorporated "best practices" into its product.

- **Partner** with other departments such as IT, Finance and Communications/Employee Relations to gain support, allies, visibility **and resources!**

And even **more lessons learned** →

- Identify your "stakeholders," **expect differences** and understand their individual (or departmental) needs.

- Employees love self-service, love the control they gain – but **may not embrace** the self-reliance as quickly as you expect or need.

- Changing existing processes alone may only result in a 15 percent savings. Seek other and new opportunities for **cost savings**.

- Do not put new technology on an old or broken process. **Get rid of inefficient processes**.

And these are
additional activities
to help you
get it done →

- Call, then **collaborate** with your professional colleagues; the HR managers, HR executives, senior executives, and employees of companies you regard highly. Ask them about what they've been able to accomplish with HR technology initiatives.

- Use **Social Media.**

- Join LinkedIn groups for HR and Technology.

- Join the professional society devoted to the use of HR technology – **IHRIM.ORG**.

*Remember, **Heroic HR** is a **mindset**, a **passion**, a delivery objective and a very achievable strategic goal.*

"The world is moved not only by the mighty shoves of the heroes, but also by the aggregate of the tiny pushes of each honest worker."

— Helen Keller

"All the world loves a hero."

— anonymous

Here is some
of Marc S. Miller
Associates'
expertise ➜

Marc S. Miller Associates: Services

- Strategic alignment of HR technology within the corporate mission/vision

- Evaluation of alternative HR technology delivery options: in-house vs. Software-as-a-Service (SaaS)

- Contract negotiations with outsourcing organizations and ASPs; definition of service level agreements (SLAs)

- Identification of HR technology performance metrics

- Needs analysis – requirements definition

- Vendor evaluation and preparation of RFI and RFP documents

- Cost justification, senior management presentations

- Strategic planning for HR technologies – implementation strategies, best practices

- Seminars, workshops, focus groups for client staff education on "The State of the HR Technology Industry"

These are
some of the
companies
Marc S. Miller
Associates
has helped →

Selected clients

- American Bar Association
- Amgen
- Bank of New York
- Becton-Dickenson
- Bell & Howell Corporation
- Burke Rehabilitation Hospital
- Cedars Sinai Medical Center
- Coactive Marketing Group
- Columbia University
- Federal Reserve Bank of Chicago
- GE Energy
- Geosyntec
- Johnson & Johnson
- Kyocera
- Los Angeles Water District
- McDonalds Corporation
- Merck
- MidSouth Bank
- New York Stock Exchange
- Nomura Securities
- Norcal Mutual Insurance
- Northwestern University
- Ohio Health
- Oxford Health Plans
- Pacificare Health Systems
- Purdue University
- Schering-Plough Corporation
- Taco Bell
- UCLA
- UniHealth
- University of Iowa
- UPS
- Westchester Institute for Human Development (WIHD)

A good first step in getting it done, and becoming **Heroic**...

Marc Miller,
president and founder, Marc S. Miller Associates

A nationally respected authority on Human Resource Information Systems, New Yorker Marc S. Miller has more than 35 years experience with all aspects of technology solutions for the function of Human Resources – including Strategy and Business Case development for In-house vs. Outsourcing decisions, Cost-Justification, Needs Analysis, Request for Proposal development and Vendor Evaluation methodologies.

Marc uses his significant industry experience and contacts to provide commentary and insight into the important trends surrounding HR Technology and HR Outsourcing. A sought after speaker, he has addressed thousands of HR Technology professionals in his participation with such organizations as the Global Oracle Human Capital Management Conference (OHUG) and a variety of HRIS vendor User Conferences, along with high visibility at most IHRIM national conferences.

He is a founding member of the New York City IHRIM Association Chapter. In 1995, he received IHRIM's highest national award, its "Summit Award" for his overall industry contributions.

He is an Adjunct Professor for HR in the MBA programs at LIU – Westchester, NY Campus and New York University - Poly Tech.

His nationwide consulting firm, his industry visibility and New Yorker attitude has made Marc Miller one of the HR Technology industry's most recognized thought leaders.

Marc S. Miller Associates
www.marcsmillerassociates.com
e-mail: marc@marcsmillerassociates.com
914 993 9697